Wedding Underwear for Mermaids

Linda Ann Strang

Honest Publishing

Wedding Underwear for Mermaids
by Linda Ann Strang
Honest Publishing

All Rights Reserved
© Copyright 2011 Linda Ann Strang
ISBN 978-0-9566658-4-3

Manufactured in the United Kingdom
Cover: 'Native Trout' by Deborah Donelson

Acknowledgements

2003	'Glissade' published in *Rain Dog*, issue 8
2006	'Mixed Media' published in *Gold Dust*, issue 7
2007	'Globalisation and the Gods of Africa' published in *Decanto*, issue 27
	'Wedding Underwear for Mermaids' published in *Other Voices*, vol. 19, no.2
	'The Man Who Married Cumulonimbus' published in *MotherVerse*, issue 6, spring 2007
	'The Hooks and Eyes of the Sun' published in *Sharp!*, vol. 5
	'Mahogany Handling', 'The Feather Saxophonist' and 'Where They Say: Don't Touch' published in *Poetry Kanto*, no. 23, 2007
	'The Grandmother at the Ends of the Earth' published in *Literary Mama*, November 2007 (online)
	'Life as an Origami Lesson' and 'Unmanned by Mother's Day' published in *Bravado*, issue 11
2008	'Hauntings with Wild Figs' published in *Barnwood Magazine* (online)
	'Marriage through the Looking Glass' published in *Niteblade* (online)
	'Ghost Husbandry' published in *The League of

Laboring Poets, vol 2, issue 4

'The Death of an Aspirin Angel', 'Roman de la Rose', 'Hail Daphne, Full of Grace', 'Marriage Season' and 'Still Life with One Ghost' published in *Cantaraville*, issue 5

'Mertopia' published in *Mythic Delirum*, issue 19

2009   'Come Live with Me in the Falling Tower' published in *Illumen*, spring 2009

'Mermaids in Aspic' and 'Charity for Nightmares' published in *Aoife's Kiss*, the former online, the latter in print, May 2009

'Magic Realists in Love' published in *A cappella Zoo*, issue 2, spring 2009

'Becoming Scottish' and 'Gwen John's Vision' published in *tinfoildresses* (online)

'Maria Nova' published in *The Catalonian Review* (online)

'Dolphin, Starred and Feathered' published in *New Fables*

'The Woman Who Became a Prayer Flag' published in *The Driftwood Review*, issue 5 (online)

'Kimono Monochrome at Midnight' published in *Electric Velocipede*, issue 19 (and online)

'Entrance Ways' published in *Flashquake* (online)

2010 'Living in the Land of Folklore' published in *Cabinet des Fees / Scheherazade's Bequest* (online)

'Middle Aged Cowboys are Women', 'Cape Infanta', and 'Protestants in Africa' published by *MLM the Quiet Press*, online and in their anthology: *Hanging by Threads*

Contents

I Ghosts

Hauntings with Wild Figs	2
Ghost Husbandry	4
Marriage Season	6
Living in the Land of Folklore	8
Roman de la Rose	10
Charity for Nightmares	12
Still Life with One Ghost	14
Life as an Origami Lesson	15
Mixed Media	17
Marriage through the Looking Glass	18
Becoming Scottish	20
Au Fait Café	22
Miscegnation for Swallows	24

II Angels in the Elements

Magic Realists in Love	28
Maria Nova: A Hymn for the 20th Century	30
Death of an Aspirin Angel	31
Come Live with me in the Falling Tower	32
Scheherazade of the Fully Automatic	34
The Feather Saxophonist	36
The Woman Who Became a Prayer Flag	38
The Hooks and Eyes of the Sun	39
Mahogany Handling	41
Middle Aged Cowboys Are Women	43
Glissade	44
The Man Who Married Cumulonimbus	45
The Grandmother at the Ends of the Earth	47

Globalisation and the Gods of Africa	49
Dolphin, Starred and Feathered	51
Protestants in Africa	53
Living with a Liberated Voice	55
Unmanned by Mothers' Day	57
Kimono Monochrome at Midnight	58

III Mermaids

Gwen John's Vision	62
Cape Infanta	64
Mermaids in Aspic	65
Memoirs of a Red Velvet Dress	67
Mertopia	69
Hail Daphne, Full of Grace: A Hymn for the 21st Century	71
Wedding Underwear for Mermaids	73
Spice Kiss	74
Where They Say: Don't Touch	75
Entrance Ways	77

I

Ghosts

Hauntings with Wild Figs

All our yesterdays dyed in the turmeric,
you're everywhere. Your family name,

Pillay, smiles gently, even from the peeling
shop fronts in museum photographs. I haunt

the framed streets of your old neighbourhood
and a phantom hand takes my life in cold Tamil.

I'm from myself apart – someone else's story –
chapters from Madras to Pondicherry.

Half-forgotten works roll over for a kiss
beneath the dust covers of my heart.

Now in sepia saris and dhotis,
what a past dances across the pub table.

You've become a boy again,
sitting in a wild fig tree in a glass of wine.

I want to taste you.
Hidden away in you is the semi-sweetness

of the answer to everything.
But, in verso flame, your spirit escapes me.

Through the window there's a low wall
that holds back the fig

and semen flavours of the sea.

Ghost Husbandry

Mei's dead children – two miscarried,
one at the age of weaning –

went to live in the chrysanthemum
blossoms near the moon gate.

When she first noticed them there
she wept and laughed with joy.

The little ones cried for milk
so she fetched her flute

and played songs for them, offering
tales of Aunty Piety the fox,

Eggborn, and the mountains.
The three boys fell asleep,

curled up above the country of flowers,
in nests of chrysanthemum clouds.

Now she goes on gardening faithfully,
even when her husband

takes a new bride – such slapping
and howls behind walls of rice paper.

Marriage Season

Her engagement ring is a crystal ball –
it glitters like a parallel universe.
They say no two are ever alike.

So she marries one, moves into her husband
the snowflake. Paired down,
she imagines her male crystal

comprises the enormity of Eurasia.
Dreamily, she consults with Baba Yaga,
admits that she too has a mortar,

keeps herself in muffs and sables,
takes the baby driving – hear the sleigh bells –
beneath the onion domes.

She enjoys the consoling iconostasis,
that gold beaten through church architecture.
The wolves howl their obeisance –

appear to run away.
Apparently the Steppes are an easy flight
to any heaven you can fancy.

Then the snowflake husband melts,
becomes a teardrop on the rose window.
She retraces herself through the prism,

notices the snowflake pattern
on her baby son's mittens. The choir breathes in,
reserving the rights to every hymn.

Living in the Land of Folklore

I remember when Rapunzel
lived with Aladdin,
magical lanterns alight in her hair,
and Goldilocks was Sindbad's lover —
so tenderly he took off her dress,
and blew her porridge cold.
Then he went away to sea
to found a heavier city of gold.

A jack-in-the-box drowned
my friend and my phoenix both,
like Henny Penny foxes, on boxing day
but Julnar consoled me –
though the Old Man of the Sea
stole the ebony horse's joystick,
and thought nothing of blowing
my hat and the goose girl
over the daisy hills and far away.

I loved you, City of the Magic Horses,
where firewood could turn into people
and people could turn into birds,
where Falada breathed *heartbreak*

even when he was dead, and Julnar
was the lovely Pomegranate of the Sea.

On her feet were sandals of sea glass
and she walked along a field of myrrh.

Roman de la Rose

The best time was in the darkness
when I couldn't tell

the cooling pink flame of my body
from the temperature of anyone else

and our house was a hand
palpitating gently. A self-contained

quiver of petals, fluid
as the feathers of a moth in chrysalis,

we were yet to part like lips,
or discover an identity – no rambling,

tuber, cabbage, or dog,
no lucrative work for an analyst.

We percolated in our liquid
Turkish delight,

a collective mouthing one scent
the way a lantern foments a light.

No hoarfrost was found
on anyone's hips.

Capillaries weren't sacrificed
to the nether thorn.

No one was singled out for grief
and no one hungered alone.

Charity for Nightmares

The troll beneath the bridge is dying
to invite someone home
to view his etchings.
If only he had a home
or some etchings.
He scratches his pustules
and dreams of art classes.

Count Dracula would
blow you kisses if he could
but his incisors are debilitating.
Necking too I'm afraid
is out of the question.
Imagine love bites
from a sabre toothed tiger.

The bloodcurdling monster
beneath the little girl's bed
would rather be under the duvet
playing with her sleeve
and listening to her breathing,
with love. Monsters are mad
about night lights that resemble

pink rabbits and quilts
that were stitched by your granny.

Even the warty witch
with her frog's egg fingernails,
sneaking into the midnight
kitchen to turn the milk sour,
has drenched herself in Chanel No. 5 –
secretly longing for valentines this year.

Would you run a bath for her?
Would you rub her back?
Shh. That's the *frou-frou*
of her switch and her broom
as she drags them along,
reluctant to leave.

Still Life with One Ghost

Place the unfinished still life before the window –
one with a view of the bay she drowned in.

Brushing aside the veils of fish she'll swim,
forward girl, through the mulberry tempest,

find the headlands of apple and pear, geranium lake,
a glass of red wine where the waves well in –

transfusion of pinotage, dark resurrection.
Washed up on the blushing cleft of a peach,

she'll lie gasping on the beach
tearing off the selkie skin of death

and you'll breach the storm caul of brush strokes,
your child reborn in the sorrows of madder,

an afterbirth of acrylics, a parody of tulips,
a diamond in the salt mines of the iris –

pages of the painted book
blasted apart by horses and spindrift again.

Life as an Origami Lesson

He had a rain jacket
that folded into a pillow.
Or was it a pillow
that folded into a rain jacket?

Take me with you, she said.
I will sleep on your pillow
and I will wear your rain jacket.
I am a girl who folds into a suitcase.

But she was a girl who folded
into baggage.
Or perhaps baggage
that folded into a girl?

And so her life went on
folding and unfolding
until, at last, at 60
she had an origami heart

that unfolded into a tapestry
of ten horned lovers. Or was it
a tapestry of ten origami lovers

that folded into a horned heart?

Mixed Media

We're quiet as a group of maquettes for coffins
from Ghana – students sketching in an art gallery,
in search of a vanishing point.

One of us takes centre stage, next to the wide-eyed
African sculptures. She announces her sadnesses
into a cell phone: an insurgent one-woman

exhibition. The crosshatching of a quarrel
patterns the back of my hand.
My fingers become a henna wedding,

then a linocut of crossed wires.
I've been assimilated by her argument.
I enter a quivering quiver tree forest,

in acrylics, trying to avoid her embarrassment
(or, more likely, being phoneless, my own).
She tells someone, in an acrylic

forest, that she doesn't care.
Soon the serigraphs and lithographs
will absorb us like somebody else's life.

Marriage through the Looking Glass

Right after I tasted the magic mushrooms
I fell into him and other nightmares.
He tied me up for twenty years
and made me view horror movies, starring,
of course in Technicolor, myself.
I played a supporting role.
Always killed off before the final girl
ran around shrieking in her torn T-shirt,
I wore my gore like an evening dress –
tanzanite, rubies, and blueberry pearls

from the heart's oozing oyster.
I didn't mind too much:
the pawns on the pornography chessboard
fawned over me; the Cheshire cat
with the preview eyes and the toupee
lent me his fake smile on Tuesdays;
and I could have my way with opium smoking
caterpillars – if I wore stilettos
and let my husband watch.

I remember my wedding day.
Do you take this ..., began the axe murderer

in his dog collar, reaching for the chain saw.
Yes, I take it, I take it, and I'll take it some more.
The baby's breath in my bouquet
burst into flames. The entire congregation
kissed my slit throat.
I gave my groom a flamingo golf club
and a wedding ring. He aimed the remote.

Becoming Scottish

I didn't know that the skeletons in my
closet wore tartan. They began with
Mac. My mother saying slyly, They think they
come from Scotland though they've been here

for years and years, had little effect. I was a princess
under the table; my concern was a handful
of broad beans in a dented soup ladle.
Being her own Tower of Babel in the kitchen,

Mother was chiefly of French and of Dutch
descent, with, perhaps, a spicy Malaysian
smack. She held a handful of cloves
and bloodlines that were none too easy to track.

By the time I strode out pouting from under the table
Mel Gibson had taken on a brotherly cast.
Robert Burns was read: I needed beating out,
and the heather in my heart was heard to cough.

Then the lassie in me came out of the cupboard;
at the culture auction she was ready to bark.
But official languages create quite a clamour

so there she was defeated under the hammer.

Now, ultimately, consider my birthright bright
a mess of curry, crowdie and custard.
I crucify the Bear on the Southern Cross,
change my heart to pomander and sniff at my loss.

Au Fait Café

After espresso, the informer
travels home with her,
rests his face between
her shoulders' angel blades.
Delicate as the aperture
that opens within a camera
set on infinity, she
succumbs to trust.
Later her chest will be the address
of explosion, eternal arrest.

With a face as soft
as leopard moths,
her trembling eyelids
find the trigger in the anther,
the tiger in the anthem,
the panther in the mantra ....
in brief, she caresses
his heart cage but he finds
his heart itself caressed.
Then she shoots him

a lowering kiss. It lifts

burning clarinet no
and yes notes,
a sacrament, a gift;
and on her own tongue –
reckless *in pace* –
the sugarless *café
au fait* taste of night.

Miscegenation for Swallows

I am a hybrid like swallows,
transforming myself as I fly:
black and white blue, black, black, black.

My passport is a page torn from the sky.
I sleep with my head under my wing,
dreaming of a homeland

where chameleon people walk through the sugar
cane of sunlight, their tongues long enough to teach
anyone. Their children are swallows in cradles.

My parents were migrant labourers, attending
the orchards of each other's hearts. Colours
flowed through them as they held hands, lost

in the pollen, their bed an equator, their tails
entwined: black and white blue, black, black, black.
They cling to the twig of their love.

I cling to their love of the twig.
I dream of having a homeland,
and my navigation point:

the latitude of starlight.

II

Angels in the Elements

Magic Realists in Love

The garden is heavy
with the bellow of bull roses.
We notice fog-horned unicorns
in the back yard.
Maria's angel runs away with the gypsies,
and she flies off –
such a blue jeans Angelus.
But what are bell bottoms for after all?

So pluck the pure string of the washing line.
Beat the olive oil drum.
Her tortillas, chillies and chocolate
could make the rock and roll mountains come.
The Holy One's metal horse is hot.
Let down your new wineskin hair.
Bring on the sexed up old wine.
Let the whole of creation tear.

See Christ of the ratchet and spanner
raise shocks at the veteran's side.
Put on your stained glass crash helmet,
Maria, God will now advise.
Fit the sprocket to the rosary.

Yes, that's right.
The way to the angel-eating quetzal
is on Guevara's motorbike
and with the way these plots are constructed
it's going to be a bumpy ride.

Have a pretzel.
She'll go down like jaguar for *agua*
when she comes down tonight.

Maria Nova: A Hymn for the 20th Century

Cubist, cross leg puzzle, Catholic radio –
when Maria started receiving raunchy country
love songs in the Dragon Café

she twisted her legs into a plait,
even so she managed to fawn multi-planar
hips from fresh air – Picasso's dove,

Braque's mandolin. She knew she had big
trouble when Confucius leapt forth from her fortune
cookie to sing, "One

singular sensation," on the table top,
shocking the restaurant with his red bowler hat,
and high-kicking ketchup all over the show.

Gabriel must have ruptured a paper lantern.
To say nothing of Raphael.

Later, those *Demoiselles* of Avignon, bless 'em,
rowed home on her broken waters – Chairman Mao's
eyes peeping from their Guernica slit and cultured wrists. **The**

Death of an Aspirin Angel

She was a powdery girl, made white, made hard,
but she rubbed my headaches away, rocked me
in her suddenly eiderdown arms.

Sometimes she came to me like an apricot
flavoured acid drop, delicious, the world
of anodyne on the tip of my tongue,

lullaby in a bottle, or even a blister. I became
the band aid's baby sister. Take your teddy,
your prayers are said, everything will be all right

in the morning. I hardly noticed the aspiring angel
was dead until the night even that matriarch, morphine
with her poppy apron, couldn't hold me down on the bed.

Come Live with me in the Falling Tower

Take the stepping stones
across the stratosphere

to the mortar arrested in collapse.
With the right amount of tension

angels make excellent suspenders,
if you fasten them here and also there.

You'll soon get over the vertigo –
flying is a bit like swimming really,

butterfly stroke works best, while doggy
paddle, quite frankly, is disastrous.

Butterflies have high blood pressure.
(So do I if I stand on my head.)

Don't worry, our demise will take decades –
time works differently here.

Terror itself is a structure – survives quakes –
with an amazing view and lots of fresh air.

You'll enjoy this penthouse, mushroom eyrie,
I swear. Some day, just for the Doppler effect,

I'll wear a red shift made of tartan stars:
I become much louder before I disappear.

Scheherazade of the Fully Automatic

She has a maxim
but she hides it in fiction –
she passes it to her children
in their football match.
Then she flutters them home
on her flying carpet
which decides to become
a welcome mat.

Her stories are castles,
comfort food,
she changes their shape
to match her intent,
pressing them together
like coconut ice,
even as she battles against
the Wizard of Rent.

She keeps *happily ever after*,
change in a teacup, defying fate
she rearranges the leaves.
She's a fluorescent lamp,
a genie coefficient,

a comic book,
Blake's tiger shake.

She hopes that, one day,
her stories will cheer them –
a travelling circus with acrobats.
She'll be dancing with mandrakes
behind the cake tins. The kids
will forget her many mistakes.
Remember instead her gingerly
proffered gingerbread embrace.

The Feather Saxophonist

When she was deflowered
it was as if the world was bereft of baby's
breath because her lover did not love her.
When they went to the fairground

together they looked into a magic mirror
that showed their hearts: he had
none, only bones bandaged in black lace;
her heart was plump with gold stars,

like the Pleiades by candlelight.
In spite of this insight, when he died
she wept. All over the place.
Now she's met a man with jazz and angel

feathers in the Palm Sunday of his hands.
When she sees him the Aretha red roses
in her soul's renaissance sing torch songs.
But she beats them down, as if roses were fire

in the violins, embarrassed
because they give her away.
Surely the saints say: Love is! Like climbing

flying stairs till you find yourself in clouds

of feathers and saxophone music
at the top - there your heart's so full of *whats*
that no-one can earth it. Forget the feather tax
on your flight plan, baby. It's worth it.

The Woman Who Became a Prayer Flag

Man and oxygen,
you are the purest atmosphere,

twisting through valleys, holding handfuls
of fabric, hair and fervent prayer.

The earth is made of cotton:
you can fly the Himalayas like a kite,

rolling the sun
on the tip of your tongue.

Even when you settle against me,
like a low cloud, for the night,

my gown whispers the ecstasy of aviation,
through frills, into your forehead;

your hand relaxes as you fall asleep,
releasing a supplication.

The Hooks and Eyes of the Sun

The boarding pass sings like a bird:
new music for mating.
Her lover, the former political prisoner,
is at the airport in Dar es Salaam –
port of peace – coming home.
In spite of the shrikes, he smiles
to hear their favourite song feathering through

the radio. She looks up from hooks and lace:
thinks of the one who was as distant as a jailbird
tortured inside the sun; there are golden archways
to paradise above the armchairs
and the collection of milk jugs is longing for milk.

She listens for his flight coming in:
her sunbird within a sunbird, crystallising above
the blushing bride proteas. Soon
the aeroplane will pollinate an alternative,
create a universe, settling a man of wandering

stars in the galaxy of her arms. Her children
run in and out of a fixed heaven. At any moment,
the sunbird will fly in through the trembling

of proteas. She unbuttons her dress and waits for him,
open – like an eye, a bride, a window.

Mahogany Handling

How human touch, wears down wood –
hands, and buttocks even.

Though gentle as woodstars,
caresses and rubbings

leave the arms and legs of hardwood –
imbuia, mahogany, teak –

slim as the limbs of hamadryads
or bleached bird bones on a beach,

angels to woody thinness
beat. There's a shaping poetry

in the unconscious everyday of hand
and second hand. Fingers

giddy as eagres change the coastline
of furniture like any force of nature:

inlaid work takes on a more delicate
air, curling waves of newborn tsunami hair,

ingrained whispers of mother of pearl,
colours of cameo, old gold locket,

the sepia shoulders of a wide-eyed girl.
So I can only wonder what power

and weather pattern your nipple wields
as it brushes against my cheek. Your glance

surely fashions me – impressionable
mahogany – forming the lusty intaglios

in the vagina's secret patina. Daily
we find the yield of the wood's honeycomb

in one another, tamer than imbuia,
your thigh and my kiss like love and teak.

Middle Aged Cowboys Are Women

Should they find a young man, bucking,
they'll show the world they're fit for the rodeo yet –
break him in, stallion bullion, between the legs.

Grit, gold nuggets, and being sheriff
are their goals; they dream of taking the law
into their hands, with a bustier to back them –

and also the high plains, the spooked desert,
the saloon with whisky, and the trigger at noon.
Jeans caked with dirt, they slick back their red hair.

Riding upon the Horsehead Nebula at night,
after a meal of black-eyed peace and coffee,
alone on the star prairie, they fall in love

with beautiful girls. They like to believe that life
is full of choice. The moon really is full
and a coyote releases its whippoorwill voice.

Glissade

She moves the children's clothes
away from the balcony door
and finds a measure of broad moonlight
between the geraniums.

She wanted to be a ballerina
before polio took over her limbs like a lover.
She lifts her arms high and tilts her head,
owns for one minute a square metre of Swan Lake;

feels invisible wings brush across her face.

The Man Who Married Cumulonimbus

When I dished up discharges, frozen peas
and hail, you always complained,
and did not like to eat
them with my forked lightning.
I never claimed to be much of a homemaker.
That doesn't matter, you would say, at first.

Face it. You just wanted to plough
a furrow through my rainbow,
with your tongue on my cumuli.
(It was the nimbus part that worried you.)
You would have agreed to anything then.
So we held onto the occluded affront of our love.

Years passed. My pre-torrential stress
meant water damage to the Persian carpets.
You started calling me thunder thighs
and our children fell
through the mists of my hands.
You're just too much, you said.

But I couldn't help it.
So I rose up, dark and tall,

blew the kitchen roof to bits,
and emigrated to the troposphere …

Now well may you try to touch the hem
of my thunderbolts, longing for the high
voltage curves of my hips and shoulders.
I can easily weather your enthusiasm.
I'll post you and the children
the salt taste of my raindrops.

Eat my fog.
When the sun reappears like oncoming traffic
through my fading cleavage
you'll know, Watson, that divorce is elemental
and I am gone.

The Grandmother at the Ends of the Earth

She beats her demons into frothy submission
with a wooden spoon and a broom,

and bakes them to keep watch at her gate
like good dogs.

She rakes together the best apple pie
with butter, nutmeg and a spanner.

When she kisses
her grandchildren they laugh forever.

The beans in her garden, full of beans, unzip
themselves and feed the multitudes.

Cocks strike
their spurs like matches and roll their own

cigarettes. Angels sneak over to the washing
line and make hammocks of the vanilla

ice cream shirts when she isn't looking.
Resting on their feathery butts,

just like the rest of us, they've left their starry hats
and coats on her black watermelons to show respect.

Globalisation and the Gods of Africa

Mujaji:
I've been crucified in a coral tree.
I bleed blue. Its flowers tear
through my tender sky tissue,
dumping their burden of umbilical umber.
A rainbow has been burnt to the colour
of bone. My complexion is penumbra.
To survey the mystery of history, when I die
I will I fly through the cells and cellulars, selling
myself - either with Vasco, Columbus, or alone.

Eshu:
Below me Africa eats itself
and its after-dinner development.
I go no higher than the moon,
but this is my evolution:
now I'm a guerrilla texting Shakespeare
to a field of stars. Text is so succulent.
I smile at it like a bracket, but the sweets
in my pocket rot my inner structure.

Lezu:
A feathered oryx, I wander the solar

system trying to forage in a vacuum;
but, finding only famine, run for the Grand
Canyon in the centre of the universe;
land and fall, a horned Icarus,
bearing wings of cocoa and tobacco.

Dxui:
At midnight I creep down the spine
of the darkness to the tempest,
a Caliban ghost with the head of a dog,
trying to shake off the accusation
of lethal petals and leaves. But sugar
breaks my bones; its serrated voice licks
furrows in my fiery flower marrow.
Sugar cancer lumps become a plantation
in my shoulder blade.

Mawu-Lisa:
You, Christ the Semi-Conductor, enfold us
like ill-fortune. We're an attachment
of skeletons. You alter us in the annealing
sea of your weal deal redemption.
We swim away in you, ether fish
with new algorithms; our final fin glimmer:
the night's last star.

Dolphin, Starred and Feathered

Tar Baby, Tar Baby, feather my tank,
belt the sirens of the land to this very day.
We told our friends the Khoisan,
in whistle opera, what would become of them
and why we'd decided to stay in the ocean.

With berry blood they painted our portraits
on the rocks of the *Maluti* mountains,
pouring watery memories into egg shells.
Their songs came back to us like desert
seeds – bruised and rootless, alone.

On wings of ostrich feathers
they had attempted flight.

Tar Baby, Asphalt Father, Mama of Bitumen,
pitch in. Heaven rests her belly on the Atlantic.
When they club us to death
we leap through the rain's navel
to swim among planets of granite.

Sometimes we dream we're the white birds
who pick all the ticks of the earth –

then our mouths vomit miracle music
and all that clockwork physic.

Dear mormyrids, keep some potential difference
for our tears in your pockets, and those electric
semaphores of yours hidden in the petal gears
of the river, every damnable and tarry night.

Protestants in Africa

I know the feel of a skin
without its animal,

circumcision rites
behind the thorn trees,

where the flint's as good
as any sterile knife,

cholera caressing the small
of your back,

heat you can drink
from the ticks in a coke bottle,

the gas long gone,
the ballistics of rocks,

and blood on the cotton,
a trading store

with its electric fan
(bladed carousel of houseflies

where every little horse
was nursed by a corpse),

the broken jawbone of a sheep
still smiling through its teeth,

and ten cents for empties.
Separated, wire by wire,

my ancestors were heretics.
God sent them to die here.

Living with a Liberated Voice

With my endless slings and slurs of accent
I could've been engendered in Kenya: prayer pitch
of fish eagle, Kilimanjaro descent cow, hide drum
rumbling below. Ella Fitzgerald revisits the cotton

field in my pharynx. Sometimes when I bump
into my voice in the street, I pretend not to know
her. I turn smiling to the costermonger, testily test

a custard apple, finger a mango, hurt myself.
Bloody prickly pear – my voice has a room
and a life of her own. Intimate of *nagapie*

and *rinkhals*, she can tongue the *iqhira*
like anyone. Bellowing down battered doors
in the shanty town at night, she's queen

of the shebeen, ululating, exaggerating,
her jazzperations. She gets home gravelly
before dawn, her eyes glowing, like fiery coals,

with vibrato. Most mornings I wake up choking,
someone else's sorrow and smoke in my throat:

her TB songbird eating the arrow:

blood in the crop and still it won't let go.

Unmanned by Mothers' Day

There's nothing less feminine than motherhood.
I'm a muscular bitch hauling children, heavy
as sacks full of filthy toweling and howling onions,
to the beds they'd rather avoid.

Though once I saw an empty tampon packet,
lying in the street, that the rain had filled
with blue gum flowers and autumn oak leaves,
even they looked like a fistful of viscera.

I hold the kids down when the dentist is hysterical,
enforce a regimen of book reading and butternuts,
stare down death when fevers laugh at paracetamol,
wage guerilla warfare against God for our survival.

No flowers, fluffy slippers, and ribbons – it's blood
and pain, vomit on my breasts, and piss.
I come in with my rifle and my shrunken heads –
gory, shell-shocked, scarred –

they hand me a gift tea cup and a pink greeting card.

Kimono Monochrome at Midnight

Her heart is a nightgown that fastens, loosely.
The throb of a nightjar slips a hand

of sound all the way down to her belly,
where an incubus is the cold ring in her navel –

stud piece of the Arctic.
Night cries want to unpick her seams,

carry her away to where her moon man
parks his Porsche – carved from a single pearl –

too close to the curb of the atmosphere,
liberate from the chain stitch and stem stitch

full-blooded nightingales for the Emperor –
in each larynx the diamond ink of starlight.

But she tightens the belt of her dreams,
waives all west of the moon

and princess possibilities that never were.
Her ears become caverns of ice candles:

a thousand sirens shrink to the failed flare
of a match. There'll be no third degree burns

for Cupid's torso tonight. Midnight slips
in through the ticking of its own keyhole,

cyan tongued as a nun in martyrdom,
needle-eyed as a daily habit.

III

MERMAIDS

Gwen John's Vision

Having stared for too long
at the impressionists,
she leaves the art museum
of her bedroom
with impressions of her own.

Two gossiping women
wobble inside a crochet of shadow.
A boy like a blur on two
blight stars, waves goodbye.
Paris is a curdle of water lilies –

choking and reflecting
on a world of deep water.
Monet paints and floats
yellow stars of saffron
from one retina to another,
from one retinue to another.

From one filly
filigree to another,
trees and riders threaten to resolve
into Seurat's *petite*

pulse points together.

Naiad of the midnight bruise,
she rubs her compound eyes
but the boy on the bicycle still
wears teasels of light everywhere
for combing her spirit through.

Cape Infanta

Where once the night of stars was tricked –
castaway trysts of amethyst,

mother-of-pearl, marsh rose,
insurgent barchans ridging the mist –

Edge of George Lilies,
part the forest.

Enter the dark,
my Bracken Caress, my Urgent Cry

of Ironwood and Milkwood,
flowering the wine cup.

Kiss of the Cove, confess the wet
laugh over wave,

the natural arch –
star tinder, estuary red in the id.

And a splash of phosphor
at the back of the head.

Mermaids in Aspic

Descending the spiral staircase
into milky paper nautilus

find Miss Mermaid's leggy immortal soul.
Rushing to her like a puppy

comes the kissing gourami
sound of the sea.

Even the souls of the afflicted
have to sleep somewhere.

Near the shores the shelly coat girls
try to call back their songs

before they're once again accused
of illicit soliciting and witchcraft.

But every mouthful of lassoing music
only makes it much worse.

The dry, preferred girls
swear they can scry sighing sirens

by simply sniffing the air.
There's a fishy smell they say:

something must be a rotten
mermaid in the state of Denmark.

Yes, the landed girls flash their damselflies
and buy on credit, while their husbands

gnash their teeth and dream
of taking Aphrodite with lemon juice,

and aspic – sea lavender on the tip of her
tongue, a salted lily in the waves of her hair.

Memoirs of a Red Velvet Dress

She's a natural birth: I fall away
like a placenta, a bolt of burgundy.
She rises up from me – Aphrodite's
chalice of merlot – to swim in the bed,
a goddess doing backstroke, breasts taut to the sky.
He licks between her legs: her latest Odyssey.
I lie on the carpet, legless, a red mermaid sister,
the tang of cigarette smoke – and drunken laughter –
drifting from the ballroom down below.
That's where he met my girl, confusing
the feel of me with the feel of her.

These days my owner's daughter tunnels
into the clench of crinkles I have become –
a prospector in a shaft of blood clots,
the burning rose of faith on her forehead –
mining for the soft inner workings of her mother,
attempting to inhale, as if the universe at once,
some maternal essence – it's non-existent.
She cannot get milk from a stale Chanel
so she nuzzles my lining for comfort,
sobs a little, nipples her thumb,
then tries on some Italian shoes,

some Jimmy Choo cloven hooves.

Moths flop about, testing my seams like cancer.
Death is a laziness I cannot resist.
Any day now I'll be demoted
from the covered hanger. Dust settles into my nap –
I haven't been worn for years.
But, perhaps, one day, some stylist or collector,
with a lisp, an asp and a feather boa,
will tip the muffs and sequins
from the bargain box, delivering me,
suffocated beetroot baby, from the charity shop.
Improve me with a pair of scissors.
Redefine me as a work of art.

Mertopia

In Mertopia a keyhole closes like a fist
against a father-husband-God's eye
and a girl keeps her secret love apple,
her green granny smith, to herself. She
unfurls her fins in the kitchen sink,
splashing bubble bath onto the martini
glasses and soup bowls.
One flick of her tail and she's on a trip:

coral lips licked, cocktails sipped,
the sea unrolling like a king sized
Japanese bed. Poseidon, sea nymphos
and nymphets at hand to serve up surf's up,
plenitude and pulchritude, with serviettes,
far from land; then – with the attraction of eight
phalluses – a man who can breathe
underwater and dive all night.

Finally, in the mood for domesticity,
she unlocks the door –makes her owl
and pearly pussycat presence felt,
with sopping footprints and rainbow hair
all over the carpets, floors, windows, walls –

while her father-husband-God indulges her,
too tame to comment or let slip
that the whole house smells of roll mops,
red herring tresses and satisfied octopus.

Hail Daphne, Full of Grace: A Hymn for the 21st Century

Kiss Daphne's peridot
fingertips, thrilling again to her
escape, celebrate the day she learned
the liberties of foliage.

But affix no Christmas stars
to our foreheads, remembering
that there are, at least,
two genocides to every story.

Rather wade through the blood
streams of the Amazon –
tree frogs on your hips,
and orchids on your eyelids.

There, whisper condolences
to the dolorous river dolphins –
their pink heads, trusting,
and resting on your shoulders.

Go back and breathe the balm of lemon
trees, healing the sick
without the usual casualty of masks

and needles. Let the woods be
oxygen tents filled with songbirds.

Celebrate your own lives
with the glade cachet of cherry
blossoms, a descant of cedars
translating the last azoic opera.

Finally, sing this hymn
as you are led through Atlantis:
Nereid, beluga, flooded is the *hortus siccus*.
Oceanid, porpoise, *ora pro nobis*.

Wedding Underwear for Mermaids

My tears fell into the pink champagne, making waves
like pinking shears. I wore every curse, gemstone,
button and pin on my bodice to make you look –
and black stockings for luck.

I'd even cut my tail in two. But you danced
out through the patio door with another girl:
the last love story knight going along for the ride.
I sank like a rock

and laughed so much to hide my bleeding heart
that the bride shook all through her honeymoon.
When we folded up the tablecloths

together, my hurt fell out of the linen like emeralds –
I had to conceal them, sparkling, in my high-heeled
shoes: my feet were mutilated all the way home.

For such I lost my last immortal tale, scale and fin.
Here. Put these in the trashcan: Hans Anderson,
Christian, the Brothers Grimm, the scallops from my
breasts: my Underwire grimace, and my Undine grin.

Spice Kiss

The pink-crinkled corolla of flesh,
palate of the strawberry sea anemone,

softer than blood coral,
right down to where the pearl stigma

releases its secret sucrose to the tongue.
Test the hardness of cardamom,

the softening of lemon zest
steamy citrus, hot and damp –

arrogating musk up, pent-up
fire at last released, incense for the dark

aside of the moon tide –
the thorn in the nerve, the tongue in the cheek.

Where They Say: Don't Touch

The river is by what it isn't,
like time:

a cry out of U-shapes,
the former lover of an oxbow lake,

a stutter of interrupted trees
out of phase,

a hum of brush music,
and a deep gouge

all the way back to the faint hope
of an under-painting.

The river's signature is a delta,
above a gold frame;

in the past, there were the open legs
of an easel.

Touch the river and kiss
it. Let it gouge out a gorge

for your dreams,

where the stars tumble in the pebbles,

rejuvenated, way down.

Entrance Ways

The first doorway:
the smile that you echo,
the craven cave image of love.

The second doorway:
the inner heart hummingbird,
beating sunlight into blood.

The third doorway:
between the split caresses
of the spilt lightning milk.

The fourth doorway:
articulated Argus eyes
on the tongue, about 101.

The fifth doorway:
the stink of prickly honey
roughing up the mouth.

The sixth doorway:
the skin sense of a fire map
unfolding from magnetic south.

Lightning Source UK Ltd.
Milton Keynes UK
UKOW040219271012

201266UK00001B/6/P